The Grief Forest

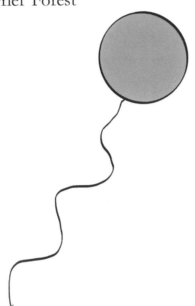

Also by Laraine Herring

A Constellation of Ghosts: A Speculative Memoir with Ravens

On Being Stuck: Tapping into the Creative Power of Writer's Block

Gathering Lights: A Novel of San Francisco

Into the Garden of Gethsemane, Georgia: a novel

The Writing Warrior: Discovering the Courage to Free Your True Voice

Ghost Swamp Blues: a novel

Writing Begins with the Breath: Embodying Your Authentic Voice

Lost Fathers: How Women Can Heal from Adolescent Father Loss

THE GRIEF FOREST

FOREST

**a book about
what we don't talk about**

LARAINE HERRING

White River Press
Amherst, Massachusetts

Published 2020 by White River Press, PO Box 3561, Amherst, Massachusetts 01004
whiteriverpress.com

ISBN: 978-1-887043-79-3 paperback
         978-1-887043-80-9 ebook

Illustrations created by the author in Procreate on an iPad Pro using Apple Pencil.

A Fierce Monkey Book

Library of Congress Cataloging-in-Publication Data

Names: Herring, Laraine, 1968, author, illustrator.
Title: The grief forest : a book about what we don't talk about / Laraine
   Herring.
Description: Amherst, Massachusetts : White River Press, 2020. | Summary:
   "The Grief Forest: a book about what we don't talk about follows the
   journey of Bunny, a young rabbit whose father has recently died. Bunny's
   grief leads her into The Grief Forest, where she meets many different
   animals who teach her important pieces of the grieving process. When she
   emerges, she understands how to work with her grief energy, and how to
   help others do the same"-- Provided by publisher.
Identifiers: LCCN 2020030526 (print) | LCCN 2020030527 (ebook) | ISBN
   9781887043793 (paperback) | ISBN 9781887043809 (ebook)
Subjects: LCSH: Grief. | Bereavement--Psychological aspects.
Classification: LCC BF575.G7 H47 2020 (print) | LCC BF575.G7 (ebook) |
   DDC 155.9/37--dc23
LC record available at https://lccn.loc.gov/2020030526
LC ebook record available at https://lccn.loc.gov/2020030527

for you

Bunny

When Bunny's Daddy died,
she captured her Grief
in a bubble
the color
of his
soul.

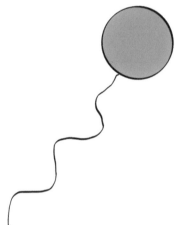

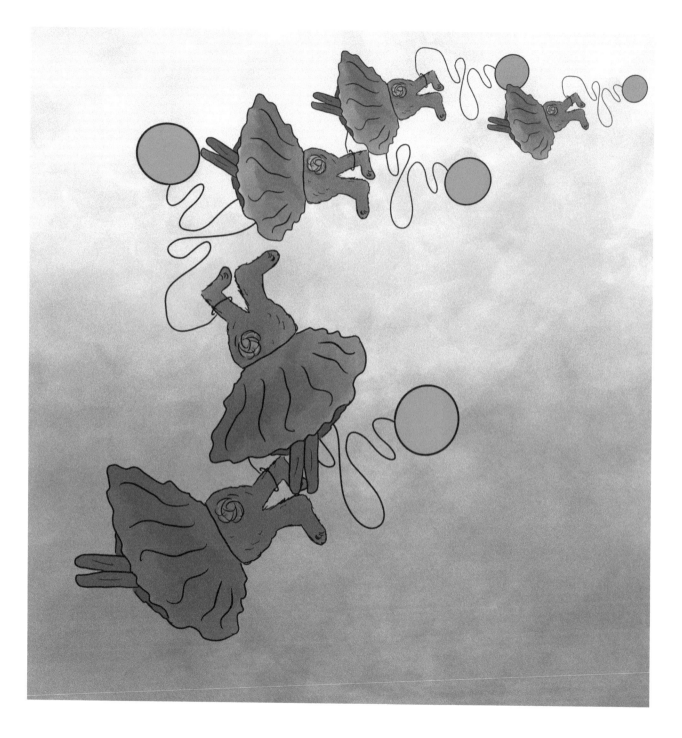

Bunny fell into a whirl of emotions and was swept away.

She arrived at the Grief Forest, holding her Grief tight.

"Welcome to the Grief Forest," crowed Raven.

Bunny noticed Raven had other Griefs in his beak
and wondered what they meant,
but she was too afraid to ask,
and she was too afraid that
Raven would take hers away,
so she hid and held it
even tighter.

Grandmother Bunny came to meet her at the edge of the Forest.

"It's OK, Bunny," she said. "I will help you."

"Why is there a fire?" asked Bunny.

She worried about the trees burning down and feeling pain.

"That's a ritual fire," said Grandmother Bunny.

"It's our sacred duty to keep it going.
It helps honor our ancestors and keeps the connection strong
between this world and the next."

Bunny gripped her Grief.

She didn't want it to go in the fire and get burned up.

"See that?" said Grandmother Bunny.
"That's Ouroboros, and he protects the Grief Forest.
The Ouroboros symbolizes the cyclical nature of the universe,
and he reminds us that life is born from death."

Bunny's eyes grew wide watching Ouroboros eating his own tail,
but she had to look away so she could focus on her own Grief.

It was getting very heavy and making her tired.

But Bunny couldn't rest because she promised she would never
put her Grief down.

It was her special chosen friend to remind her of Daddy.

Sometimes she even talked to her Grief.

That made her feel less lonely, and she could pretend
she was talking to her father.

They arrived at a circle in the Forest
where many bunnies waited with their own Griefs.

"Let's join them," said Grandmother Bunny.
"They've been waiting for us."

Bunny trembled.

"Don't be afraid," said Grandmother Bunny,
but Bunny couldn't help it.

There was so much Grief in the circle,
she didn't know how
she would breathe,
so she ran away and
came face to face with
Death,
holding its own
Grief on a string.

Bunny waited for Death to speak, but it didn't.

Death held up a lantern, and Bunny decided to follow the light, even though it took her away from Grandmother Bunny and deeper into the Forest.

Ghosts were everywhere.

Bunny realized every Ghost carried a different color of Grief.

Were there other kinds of Grief besides hers?

Hers was so big it felt like the only one in the world.
But maybe others had experienced Grief, too?

Her curiosity was almost bigger than her fear.

Almost, but not quite.

"Follow me," said Death.

Death summoned Bunny's Grief toward it,
and Bunny had to follow quickly,
so she didn't lose track of it.

"Are you ready to meet Grief?" asked Death.

Bunny thought she had met Grief.
She carried it with her everywhere she went.

"Carrying a thing and understanding a thing
are not the same," said Death.

"Many creatures think this,
but that confusion makes living hard."

Bunny was surprised that Death had compassion for others.

That went against the story she had been told
about the meaning of Death.

"If you want to know Grief's secrets, you have to follow me,"
said Death. "But I am going into the cave whether you are with me
or not."

Grandmother Bunny had stayed with the other bunnies
in the Grief Circle.

Bunny waved to her, but she was busy reading from a big book.

Bunny didn't want to walk with Death,
but she also didn't want to be alone with her Grief,
so she gathered up her courage and entered the cave.

The first creatures she met were two startled kittens.

"Grief catches you by surprise, sometimes," said Death.
"Before you know it, you can float away and get lost."

Bunny could relate to that.

When she first got her Grief, it had a mind of its own,
and all she could do was hold on.

"Shhh," said Death.

Solitary Cat watched the falling leaves.

She was so still! "What is she doing?" asked Bunny.

"She is not doing at all," said Death. "She is being."

Bunny didn't understand what that meant,
and Death didn't say anything else.

Bunny thought she was supposed to do things all the time
in order to be a good Bunny.

She had been doing a lot when her Daddy died,
and her Grief found her.

But soon after, she started to do even more
because it was what she knew.

She was also sure that if
she stopped moving,
she would have
died, too.

28

The next creature looked so strange!

"What's wrong with them?" asked Bunny.

"Nothing at all," said Death. "Ask them what's happening."

The creature laughed nervously, but said,
"I feel like nothing fits! I'm in so many different skins."

"Grief breaks you apart," said Death.
"And it is scary sometimes when you're in between
who you were and who you're becoming."

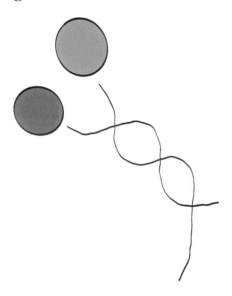

When Bunny saw the melted snow, she felt sad.

All that was left was a carrot nose.

"I thought I had prepared," said the one who was left behind.

"I knew she would melt,
but I was still so surprised
by the heat of the sun."

"It's natural to anticipate feeling sad," said Death.
"That's one way creatures try to cope."

Bunny's Daddy had been sick for a very long time,
and Bunny had done the same thing.

She had practiced what she would do when he died,
but it hadn't changed his dying.

"It's OK," said Death.
"You didn't do anything wrong, but neither did I.
The sun always sets on schedule."

"Can you help me?" said Floppy Bunny.
"I seem to have gotten stuck in my memories."

Bunny went to go untangle the strip of defining moments,
but Death stopped her. "They aren't yours to unravel."

"How do I help, then?" she asked.

Floppy Bunny was so wrapped up in the past,
she was afraid he would strangle himself.

He kept watching the same scene over and over again.

"Ask him to tell you the story of that scene," said Death,
"and when he's done, just say 'thank you'."

That didn't seem like it would be enough to help Floppy Bunny.

He was so tightly wound.

"You would be surprised," said Death.
"Telling important stories untangles many knots."

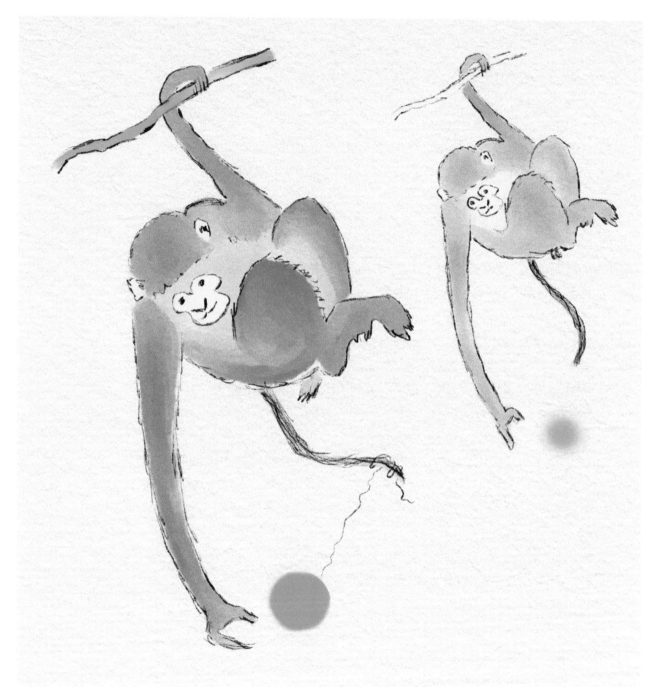

Monkey was trying so hard to touch her friend.

"Will she ever reach her?" asked Bunny.

"No. The old ways of connecting will no longer work," said Death.

"Then why does she keep doing it that way?"

"Because it's familiar," said Death. "And because she wants so very much to be able to find her again."

Bunny was overwhelmed with sadness,
so she did what she always did
when she felt too many feelings.

She held Grief even closer.

Maybe she was reaching, too, like Monkey,
and every time her Daddy didn't reach back,
her Grief grew thicker.

"How can we fix it?" she asked,
but Death had gone quiet again,
watching.

When Death and Bunny approached the Elephants,
they were deep in conversation.

"I'll wait for you," said the living Elephant.

The ghost Elephant didn't say anything,
but she wrapped her trunk tighter
around the living Elephant's trunk.

Maybe Bunny should have wrapped her ears
around her Daddy's ears.

"Are they stuck?" asked Bunny.

"They are finding a new way to relate to each other," said Death.
"A way where they can be connected but not entangled.
It requires a new way of loving."

Bunny didn't understand the difference between
connected and entangled.

They looked the same to her.

Moon Monkey sang a song as she looked to the night sky.
"There is so much I still want to say to you, beloved.
We didn't even get to say good-bye."

Bunny thought of her future
and all the things
she wouldn't be able to tell
her Daddy.

She'd believed there would always be one more day.

Her Grief began to tug at its string,
and Bunny was sure she heard it rumbling.

Was it alive?

Did it have something to say?

She thought she saw Death smile,
but it was so hard to tell what was happening
underneath that hood.

They continued deeper into the Forest and met Fox.

He was hard to spot.

"Grief can make you feel invisible," said Fox.

"The whole world keeps happening all around you
like nothing has changed."

Bunny's Grief grew louder.

It was so loud, Fox heard it and scampered off into the trees.

The noise scared Bunny.

She was afraid of what Grief wanted to say,
so she
swallowed
it.

Robin sat staring at her bright blue egg.

It was so pretty and perfect.

Death brushed its hand over the egg, and Robin shivered.

Bunny started to say something, but Robin's Grief blew towards her and she backed away.

"My egg didn't hatch," said Robin. "Even though I did everything right."

Bunny loved watching the new birds in the spring.

Why would Death want a baby bird?

"Did you take her egg?" asked Bunny.

She was so angry! Death was too greedy. It couldn't just go around taking anything it wanted.

"I don't take," said Death. "But I know it looks like that to you."

"What do you do then?" asked Bunny.

Death turned away. "What I must."

"It takes so much energy to keep my Grief stuffed in a box,"
said Spider Monkey.

Bunny nodded, but kept her mouth closed so Grief wouldn't get out.

If she squeezed

and squeezed

and squeezed her lips together,

she could hold it

down.

Bunny noticed two Alligators!
One stared into the swamp,
and another one reflected underneath him.

"One Grief can release older Griefs,"
said the Alligator on the swamp's edge.
"When you meet an older one, it's best to say hello."

Bunny did not want to say hello to anything from the dark,
so she ran to her safe hiding place.

"Grief is cumulative," said Alligator's reflection.

His tail splashed the swamp,
and the Griefs rippled orange and blue.

"It builds up inside if you don't express it
when you feel it."

He opened his mouth wide.

"You might think you've resolved something,
but old sorrows can still surprise you
in the dark."

Bunny was so tired, and the Alligators had scared her.

Her jaw hurt from holding her Grief inside,
and her Grief had taken up so much space,
it was making her bones hurt
and her stomach gurgle.

She looked for Death, but it had wandered off.

Bear yawned.

"Grief is a stress response. Rest is best."

When Bunny thought about lying down, her whole body contracted.

If she went to sleep, she couldn't keep track of her Grief.
It might float away, and she would wake up alone.

She decided it was best to keep moving.

Bunny remembered Solitary Cat.

Silence is so loud, she thought.

Lynx heard her thoughts, and said, "Don't be afraid of emptiness.
Let the wind blow through you."

Lynx had three Griefs bouncing nearby.

Those Griefs were different. They didn't have any strings!
Lynx stretched out a paw to bat at one of them,
and the Grief soared.

"Oh no!" said Bunny.

"Your Grief is going to disappear!
If it does, what will happen to you?
Who will you be?"

Lynx did not reply.

A sneaker wave caught Bunny and pulled her into the ocean.
Bunny was sure her Grief was all that kept her afloat,

so she held on for her life

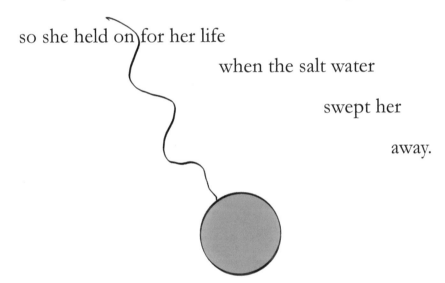

when the salt water

swept her

away.

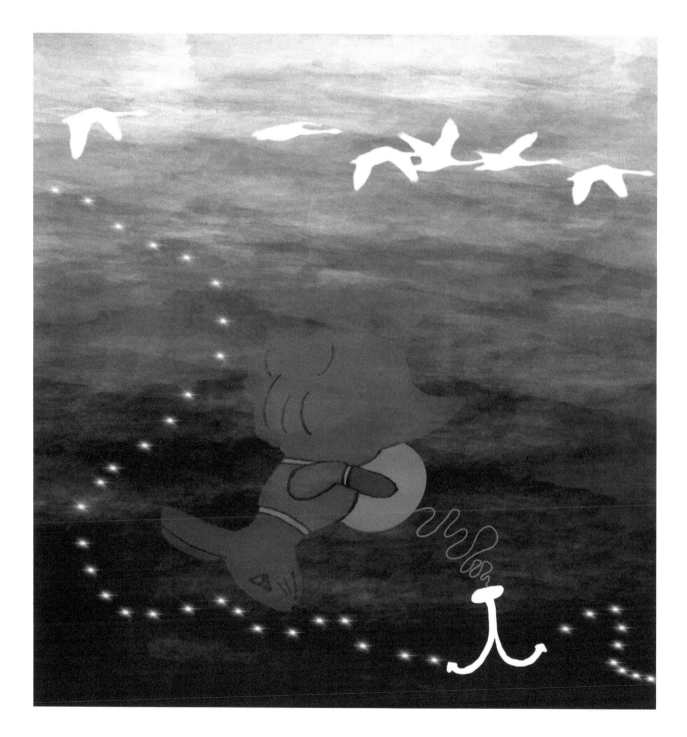

But she gripped so tightly, she couldn't tell where Grief ended and she began.

Grief became so heavy in her belly that Bunny started to sink.

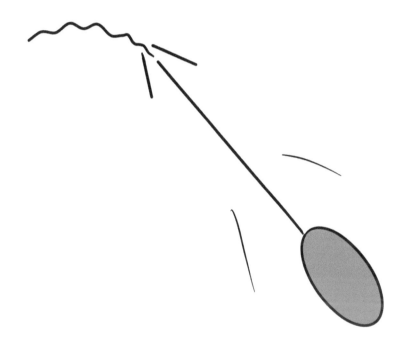

On her way under the sea, she passed Whale on the shore.

Her belly was filled with Grief, too.

"Oh my," said Whale. "I swallowed all my Grief and beached myself.
Now I can't breathe."

Bunny noticed a Grief was stuck in Whale's blowhole,
but when she tried to free it,
a rip tide pulled Bunny deeper under.

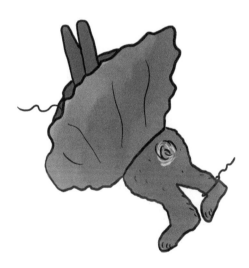

As she sank further, she met Octopus,
who glowed with many different colors.

"I have three hearts!" said Octopus. "One for loving myself,
one for loving others, and one for loving the ocean."

Bunny wasn't sure how to keep her own single heart safe.
She was glad she didn't have to take care of three!

Then, Octopus showed her how he could change his
appearance based on his surroundings.

That could be useful, thought Bunny,
but if she changed too much,
how would her Grief recognize her?

How would her Daddy find her?

"Grief teaches us to live with uncertainty," said Octopus.
"It also requires us to change our skins."

But Bunny didn't hear him.

She was already tumbling to the ocean floor.

When Bunny's paws hit the sand, she bounced up and emerged
into a bloom of shimmering Jellyfish.

They were so beautiful! She opened her mouth for just a minute,
and a little bit of her Grief slipped out and began to pull her up.

She'd forgotten to hold her breath!

She panicked and gulped and gulped and gulped
to try and recapture her Grief fragment,
but it had already escaped.

Each time she gulped, a little more Grief swam out.

"There is value in less effort," said Pink Jellyfish.
"Trust the current of your emotional tide to take you to shore."

That made no sense to Bunny, but she didn't have time to
think about it because the current had carried her Grief away,
and she had to get busy chasing it before it traveled too far.

Without realizing it, Bunny had floated closer to the water's surface.

She was relieved to see her Grief waiting for her in a school of Koi.

"Don't move faster than you can feel," said Orange Koi.

More riddles, thought Bunny,
but something in the back of her mind stirred.

She captured her Grief again, but when she tried to swallow it,
it had grown too big for her mouth.

Bunny had no choice but to keep her Grief outside of herself.

She would simply have to be more careful not to lose track of it.

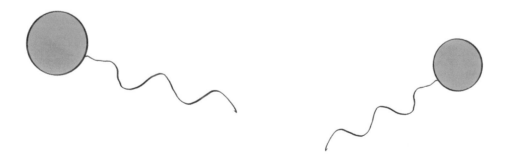

As Bunny neared the surface, she passed Bullfrog sitting on a lily pad.

"Amphibian means two lives," said Bullfrog.

"Grief teaches you a new way to breathe."

Bunny's Grief had taken on its own life now,
and it dragged Bunny up through the water
into the dark, dark Forest.

Bunny panted, and as she gasped for breath,
her Grief moved back and forth
with her inhales and exhales.

How would she get back to Grandmother Bunny?

It was so dark, and she was so alone.

Even Death had abandoned her.

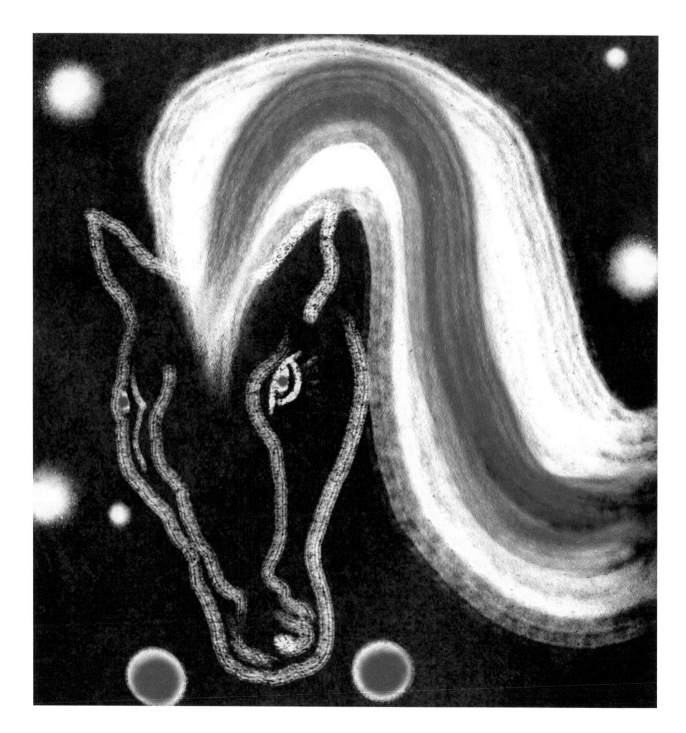

"Sometimes you can't see the light you carry until you are in the dark," said Horse.

Bunny was startled and only saw a glimmer of Horse before she was swallowed by the night.

Next, Bunny saw three Bats hanging upside down.

Their hearts glowed.

"When you enter a dark place," they said in unison,
"it is useful to make friends with the creatures who live there."

"How do I make friends with creatures so different from me?"

"You need to find the ways you're the same," said the Bats.

Wolf came out of nowhere, his silver coat shining in the moonlight.

"Hello," said Wolf. "Welcome to my house."

Bunny was too scared to say anything back.
The darkest part of the Forest did not look like
any house she recognized.

Wolf chuckled.

"If you try to make your new life
look like your old life, you'll be lost.
Grief is its own world."

Bunny's Grief let out a yelp, which made Wolf howl at the moon.

"All I want is things to be like they were before,"
Bunny said, and a hot tear sprang to her right eye.

Grief's cries grew louder.

"I know, Bunny," said Wolf. "But they will not."

"I heard your Grief," said Owl. "Here I am."

Owl turned his head almost entirely around.

"Why do you do that?" Bunny asked.

"I'm able to see where I've been and where I'm going," said Owl.
"I'm not stuck looking in only one direction."

"I don't understand," said Bunny.

"You need to bring what will help you
from the past into your present and future,
without looking back so much that you fall out of the sky."

Bunny remembered Floppy Bunny.
He was so tangled up in his memories that he'd become a cocoon.

"Don't be deceived," said Owl.
"The Dark is not the absence of Light.
The Dark uses Light in a different way, that is all."

Snail crept across the path, leaving a glistening trail behind her.

"There is always light in the Grief Forest," said Snail.

"Even if it is far away."

Bunny wanted to give up. She was exhausted and her
Grief was out of control, crying and yelping and tugging at its string.

Death had left her. Grandmother Bunny had promised to help her,
but she was gone, too.

She decided she would sit beneath a tree
with her Grief and wait it out.

Her Grief got tangled up in Spider's web,
and its struggle to break free woke Spider up.

"Oh, Bunny," Spider said, as she gently separated
the strands of her web so Grief could escape.
"Time doesn't heal anything. Time simply passes.
Until you acknowledge your wounds, they fester and grow."

Bunny's Grief sighed, and Bunny was confused.
Didn't her Grief want to be with her?

She closed her eyes, but her Grief leapt up and down,
its sounds forming two words she had come to dread.

"Follow me."

The path was pitch black.
Snail had gone. Owl had gone. Wolf had gone.

It was so dark, Bunny's Grief was swallowed up in it,
and she wasn't sure she was going in the right direction at all.
And then, one by one, Fireflies emerged
in strands from the trees to illuminate the path.

"When you're in the darkest part of the Forest," they said,
"your ancestors will come and light the way."

Bunny's heart felt warm for the first time since Daddy died,
and it wasn't beating nearly as fast.

Was Daddy a Firefly, too?

Maybe Daddy wasn't Grief at all, and Bunny had gotten lost
trying to make this world look like her old world.

With each step, more Fireflies appeared.
Bunny could see her Grief, but it was much farther down the path.

She watched it for a full minute
before she remembered she was supposed to hold it close.

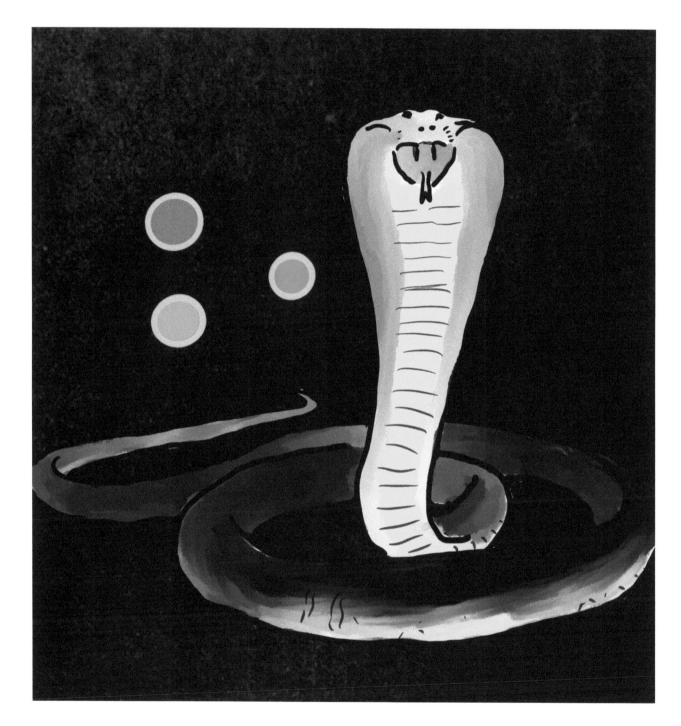

Cobra rose up from the Forest floor, and Bunny screamed.

Cobra's hood reminded her of Death.
Bunny crouched down and waited to die.
Cobra wrapped himself around her and whispered in her ear,
"Why are you afraid of me?"

Bunny didn't know.
All her life she was told that Death was bad
and Cobra was bad
and Dark was bad.
Anger was bad.
Sadness was bad.
All feelings that weren't nice were bad.

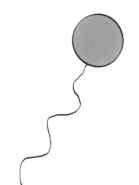

"But why do you think that?" asked Cobra.
The cool smoothness of his scales soothed her, and she relaxed.

"It's just what I was told," she admitted.

Cobra unfurled and stretched tall. "You might question why
you have been taught to fear the things you don't understand,
instead of taking the time to greet them. It's frankly very rude."

Bunny's Grief had become so excited listening to Cobra that
it was spinning around the sky.

Cobra returned to the darkness,
and Bunny sat on a stump and
decided to invite her Grief to join her.

"What do you need?" she asked Grief,
and Grief was so glad to be spoken to, she cried,
which made Bunny cry,
and then they laughed a little bit
and became quiet and watched the stars.

"I've been lonely," said Grief.
"You captured me instead of getting to know me."

"I was afraid that if I didn't attach to you, I would lose my Daddy."

Grief held Bunny close while she cried,
and when Bunny had finished,
Grief released her.

"That's not how it works," said Grief. "Look!"

Many bunnies with many colors of Grief floated in the
sky among the stars.

"Every bunny has their own Grief,
and their Grief has a special power that's only for them.
But you can only find out what yours is if you take the time to ask."

"Will you tell me what my power is?" asked Bunny.

Death tapped her on the shoulder before Grief could answer.

"You scared me," said Bunny.

Death wound its Grief string around its fingers.
"I seem to always do that."

"What is my power?" she asked again.

"How are you different since your daddy died?" asked Death.
"The way you've changed holds the secret to your new power."

Bunny scrunched up her nose to think.

Her breathing was smoother.

Her whiskers twitched.

"I feel lighter," she said.

"That is a start," said Death. "Shall we walk on?"

Mouse was so tiny, Bunny almost missed her.

She was surrounded by the strangest Grief trees.

"What happened to you?" asked Bunny.

"Every time I tried to talk about my Grief, my friends told me not to be sad," said Mouse. "They said I should be grateful for what I have. But that makes me feel guilty because I am grateful, but I'm also sad, so I don't know what's OK to say. I walk on pins and needles around them and make myself as small as I can, so they'll still want to be near me. I don't want to be alone."

Death shook its head. "Bypassing a feeling is not a shortcut. Don't let anyone tell you that you can only feel one thing at a time. You can be both sad and grateful."

"I see your Grief!" Bunny blurted out. "Mouse! I see it!"

"You do?" said Mouse.

"I do!"

Mouse smiled and grew bigger, and Bunny felt good inside. Somehow meeting Mouse's Grief had brought them closer.

"Thank you," said Mouse, and a new joy touched Bunny's heart.

94

Panther waited for them on a cliff's edge.
The sun cast a panther-sized shadow beside him.

Bunny didn't understand how there was suddenly sun
when it had been so dark.

Did everything exist at once?

The Grief Forest didn't work the same way as her other life had.

"There is no more other life," said Panther.
"But now you know.
Shadows cannot exist without light.
Grief is multifaceted.
Don't forget and get trapped in the dark.
Nothing is permanent."

The Forest had opened up, and Death and Bunny were in front of the entrance to Grandmother Bunny's house.

"Are you ready to go inside?" asked Death.

Bunny asked her Grief if it was time, but her Grief said not yet.

There was one more thing to do.

When Bunny released her Grief to the sky,
the purest part of it turned into love
and nestled inside her heart.

Her Grief had become so much love
that her heart stretched bigger,
but it did not break.

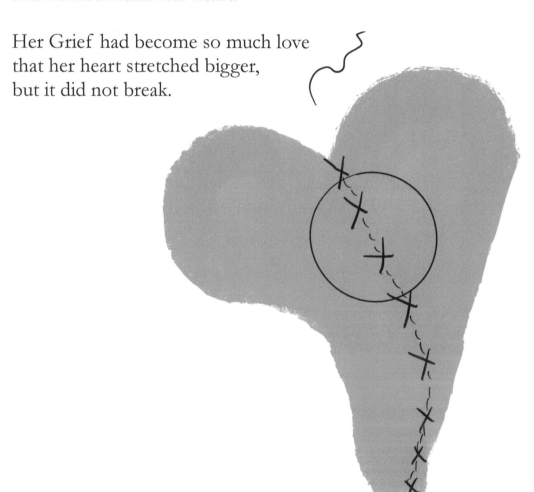

"Where is my Daddy?" asked Bunny.

"I don't know," said Death, holding its own Grief close. "I'm just the transportation."

"What is your Grief?"

Death was quiet, and then said, "My Grief is disconnection. People treat me like I am not a part of Life."

Bunny slipped her paw into Death's hand, and they sat together for a long time in the new dawn.

Bunny touched a pouch that was tied around her neck with a string.

Where had it come from, and why hadn't she felt it?
It rested right above her heart.

Maybe her heart had been so walled off, it stopped being able to feel.
She opened the bag and gasped.

"Oh! I think I have a part of all the creatures I met in the Forest!
Here's a feather, a scale, a tooth, and a piece of silk!
There's so much more, too!"

"We're a part of everyone we meet," said Death.

"Now look up, or you will miss the sunrise."

"I'm sorry you're so lonely," said Bunny.

"Thank you for talking to me," said Death.

And that's when Bunny understood her Grief Power.

"I have to go," she said.

Death nodded. "I do, too."

"Welcome back!" said Grandmother Bunny.

This time Bunny entered the Grief Circle without fear.

She told all the bunnies about her adventures in the Grief Forest, and every word made her feel connected.

Her Grief came with her, but it wasn't on a string anymore.

It hovered nearby, coming and going as it pleased.

Grandmother Bunny took Bunny's Grief
and added a piece of it to her book.

"Your storytelling power can help other bunnies,"
she said.

"When we read from the Big Book of Grief Stories,
we feel less alone."

Bunny was enchanted by the rainbow of colors
playing with each other in the clouds.

The Grief that marked Bunny had turned into
a source of light inside of her.

She couldn't always see it, but she felt it.

Her Grief, now free, laughed and spun in the air.

"Isn't it magical?" said Grandmother Bunny.

When Bunny saw how happy
the energies were without strings,
she understood something important.

Every feeling had a purpose,
and every feeling had something it needed to say.

"We can see your light now," said Grandmother Bunny.

"Take care of it so it always glows and doesn't get hidden.
Other bunnies will need to see it
when they are lost in the Grief Forest."

I love you, Bunny!

Daddy

Bunny watched all the Griefs streaking the sky.

Death's Grief played there, too,
and she smiled and hoped Death found a new friend
to walk with in the Forest for awhile.

Then Bunny remembered something her Daddy had said
a long time ago,
back before he got so sick
and flew away.

Her light pulsed with Daddy's voice-memory,
but it was a warm feeling this time,
and it didn't steal her breath.

"Don't try to capture love, Bunny.
It will shrivel and die if you hold it.

Love expands wider than you can imagine,
and if you can let it go,
it will fill the whole sky."

A Word About Grief

Grief is the natural response to a change of any kind. Healthy grieving is not about "getting over" something. It is not about forgetting who or what we loved. Healthy grieving allows the natural expression of the myriad of feelings we may have when we experience a loss to move through us in a safe manner.

Grief is not limited to mourning a death. Yes, we grieve others' passing, but we also grieve places we miss, dreams that never materialized, missed opportunities, pets that we no longer have, the climate we remember, illnesses, and much more. Grief can be overpowering, or it can be stealthy. It can be oppressive, or it can lightly touch us at the most unexpected times. Grief can manifest in a variety of forms, such as tears, rage, depression, self-harm, aggression, addiction, workaholism, silence, withdrawal, and detachment. Grief can be delayed, absent, prolonged, and anticipated. Grief doesn't have a clear start and stop time. There is no statute of limitations on its expression. It isn't a pathology or an experience to be ashamed of or deny. It is a facet of the vast emotional range of the human being.

Complicated grief is grief that is characterized by anger, resentment, intense yearning for the object of attachment, or avoidance of any reminders of the loss. In *The Grief Forest*, Bunny is experiencing complicated grief. She responds to the death of her father by immediately clutching to her grief and denying that it can evolve, and over time, she identifies with her grief and begins to lose her own agency.

None of us grieve in the same ways. Our cultural, societal, and familial landscapes inform our initial approaches to grief. Most of us did not receive great instruction on working with grief. It has the distinction of falling into one of the "undesirable" categories of human emotion, and therefore, it is to be avoided, or at the very least, moved through as quickly as possible. It is certainly not something to talk about too much, lest we alienate the very people we lean on for support.

No emotion is "good" or "bad". Emotions simply *are*, and all of them serve a purpose for our psychological health. We may not know how to effectively use the ones we've ignored or been afraid of, but that doesn't mean we can't learn.

If you're feeling stuck like Bunny, a therapist might be useful for you. Although therapy isn't a good fit for everyone, all of us need help from others from time to time, and the grief response has a built in mechanism to help us do this. Oxytocin, one of the stress hormones released when we grieve, is a hormone that encourages us to be social. Seeking and providing support is an act of love, and Grandmother Bunny is right when she says, "When we read from the Big Book of Grief Stories, we feel less alone."

Meeting our grief allows us an unexpected freedom that occurs when the energy we've been expending avoiding it is released. Feeling our grief won't bring back what we've lost. Nothing will. If we love, we grieve, but that grief has the potential to open our hearts in profound ways and provide a wisdom earned on no other path.

Thank you for joining Bunny on her journey. We wish you the deepest love.

Author's Note

Thank you to Dalena Watson, for twenty years of journeying and working with hidden things; Rick Hamilton, for art direction; Linda Roghaar, for saying, "I think this is a book!"; and Keith Haynes for seeing every animal I drew with love.

Grieving is a part of living and loving. As long as I can remember, I have been drawn to the energy of grief and sorrow. At times, they pulled me under, but in doing so, I learned to swim. I learned how to alchemize grief and how to respect it and allow its natural expression. I had to unlearn many things I internalized from a variety of sources: don't cry; other people have it worse; there are plenty of fish in the sea; at least your father loved you; crying is ugly; when you are sad, people leave you; pretending everything is OK is the secret to finding companionship; no one will love you if you're so sad all the time; girls don't get angry; anger is bad; sadness is bad; be happy; work hard. Perhaps you can add your own internalized messages to this list.

With each story I unraveled, I learned something new. I began to see how these patterns had been passed down, generation to generation, and how they were survival strategies that had turned toxic. I saw how the energy I took avoiding things and fighting them is energy I couldn't use for creating things, for loving others, and for caring for myself.

This book has whispered to me for years, but I dismissed it for a variety of reasons. The biggest resistance I faced is that I am not a trained artist. But the book kept at me until I had no choice but to follow the lines. I began to doodle bunnies, and as Bunny emerged, so did all the animals from her Grief Forest. For each animal, I asked it what it represented and what energy it wanted to convey, and then I tried to capture that feeling in the illustration and to provide simple language for it in the text. The animals grow, as Bunny grows, from grievers into guides, and each animal brings a necessary reflection and observation on the grieving process.

Bereavement is a noun. It is a place. Grief is the internal expression of sorrow, and mourning is its external expression. When we grieve, we enter the state of bereavement. I wanted to create a metaphor for that noun and a place that mirrors the confusion, wonder, despair, and hope of the liminal period of bereavement. The Grief Forest is that place. I hope it provides insights and comfort, and above all, a safe space in which to feel.

For more information and resources, please visit griefforest.com.

Photo Credit: MH Ramona Swift

Photo Credit: Keith Haynes

Laraine Herring holds an MFA in Creative Writing and an MA in Counseling Psychology. She has worked as a grief counselor for children and families, with a focus on narrative medicine and play therapies. Her fiction won the Barbara Deming Award for Women, and her nonfiction has been nominated for a Pushcart Prize. Her work has appeared in *The New York Times, Tiferet, K'in, The Manifest-Station,* and many other places. Her first book, *Lost Fathers: How Women Can Heal from Adolescent Father Loss*, was released in 2005 from Hazelden. Other books include a trilogy of writing guides from Shambhala: *Writing Begins with the Breath; The Writing Warrior;* and *On Being Stuck: Tapping into the Creative Power of Writer's Block.* Her memoir, *A Constellation of Ghosts: A Speculative Memoir with Ravens,* is available from Regal House. She is a tenured professor of psychology and creative writing and lives in northern Arizona. laraineherring.com